J
796.8   Neff, Fred
Ne   Karate is for Me

KARATE

is for me

KARATE
is for me

Fred Neff

photographs by
James E. Reid

 Lerner Publications Company Minneapolis

To my father and mother, who have shown me love, kindness, and understanding through the years

LIBRARY OF CONGRESS CATALOGING IN PUBLICATION DATA

Neff, Fred.
  Karate is for me.

  (A Sports for Me Book)
  SUMMARY: A young girl describes her experiences in learning beginning karate techniques including stances, blocking,
punching, kicking, and basic kata movements.

  1. Karate—Juvenile literature. [1. Karate] I. Reid, James E.
II. Title. III. Series.

GV1114.3.N445   796.8'153   79-16900
ISBN 0-8225-1090-1

Manufactured in the United States of America.
Published simultaneously in Canada by J. M. Dent & Sons
(Canada) Ltd., Don Mills, Ontario.

International Standard Book Number: 0-8225-1090-1
Library of Congress Catalog Card Number: 79-16900

1 2 3 4 5 6 7 8 9 10 90 89 88 87 86 85 84 83 82 81 80

Hello. My name is Becky. I am studying karate and I really love it. Karate is an ancient Asian art of self-defense. The word **karate** means "empty hand" because students of this form of self-defense do not use weapons against attackers. Instead, we use a variety of punches, kicks, and throws.

I first became interested in karate when my mother and father began to study it. I watched them practice at home. I wanted to try some of the moves, too. But Mom and Dad said the karate moves were not as easy as they looked. I could hurt myself or someone else if I did not perform the moves

correctly. So my parents enrolled me in a beginning karate class taught by a qualified instructor.

My karate class is held in a large gym. At the first lesson, we met Mr. Miller, our instructor. He told us to sit down with our legs crossed and our backs straight. Then he talked to us about karate.

Mr. Miller said, "I will be teaching you moves that can be used in self-defense. But karate is more than just fighting. Karate involves mental training, too. We will be more concerned with perfecting our moves than with actual fighting. You will gain confidence because you will know that you are able to defend yourselves."

Next Mr. Miller told us about his karate uniform. It is called a **gi** (GEE). A gi is loose and comfortable, so your arms and legs are free to move. Mr. Miller said that we should all have a gi for our next class.

We began our karate training with some exercises. Mr. Miller said we would be able to perform better if our muscles were warm and loose. We warmed up by stretching. I learned the **front bending exercise** and the **side stretch.**

We warmed up our leg muscles with the √**two-leg stretch**. For this exercise, I stood with my feet apart. Then I slowly spread my legs and lowered myself to the floor.

My muscles were really stiff. At my first lesson, I could not stretch very far. It would take a lot of practice before I became flexible enough to touch my legs to the floor.

Another exercise that helped my legs loosen up was the **leg kick**. It was hard for me because I had trouble lifting my leg up high. Mr. Miller told me to relax and concentrate. Soon I could kick higher and harder.

After our class was warmed up, Mr. Miller taught us our first karate technique. It was a basic self-defense **stance**, or standing position. A strong stance is important because it prepares you to defend yourself. Your stance will help you keep your balance. A stance is the starting position for all kicks, punches, dodges, and blocks.

We learned the **modified horse stance**. It is called this because your legs are spread and slightly bent as if you are riding a horse. One leg is placed in front of the other. Your weight is even on both legs. Your hand positions are important, too. One hand is stretched in front of the body. The other hand is at your side. This hand is in a fist, palm facing up.

13

One of the moves you can do from the modified horse stance is the **rising block**. This block guards against attacks to your head or chest. To do the rising block, swing your forward arm up in front of your head. The soft part of your forearm should face out. As you swing the arm up, it will block an attacker's punch or kick.

14

The rising block is often followed with a **forefist punch**. Two or more moves used together like this are called a **combination**.

The forefist punch is started with the rear hand in a fist. To make a proper fist, fold your fingers tightly into your palm. Then place your thumb across the folded fingers.

To throw the punch, move your fist forward. At the same time, twist your fist so

the palm faces down and your knuckles face up. You should hit your target with the first and second knuckles of your fist.

As we practiced the block-punch combination, Mr. Miller told us to imagine a powerful aggressor in front of us. By concentrating on this, we could put more power into our moves. It really worked.

Next we practiced the block-punch with a partner. Mr. Miller cautioned us to control all of the punches we throw. "Be careful not to hit someone accidentally or put too much power behind a punch at a partner," he said. "It is also not wise to use karate outside the class unless you need to defend yourself in an emergency."

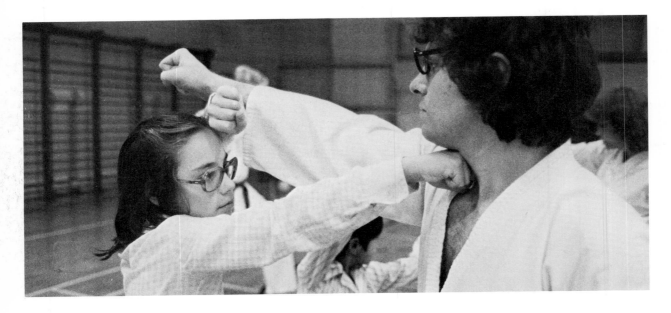

The next part of the evening was very exciting. Mr. Miller showed us a **kata**. A kata is a series of karate moves, which are performed as if you are defending yourself from an imaginary attacker. Mr. Miller's movements flowed smoothly without interruption. He looked like a graceful dancer.

The kata showed how karate moves can be linked together. Mr. Miller said self-defense moves are most effective when done in combinations like these. That is why students must learn and practice combinations from the very beginning of their karate training.

At the end of class, we did the **final bow**.

This is a sign of respect for one another. Then the class was over.

Some of the students stayed after class to talk. I felt better when I heard them say that they were having trouble doing some of the exercises, too. We were tired but happy. Everyone was excited about the beautiful kata we had seen.

I began looking forward to my next karate class. That was an extra-special day because I wore my new gi. It was nice and loose. I felt very comfortable in it when I did my stretching exercises before class.

At class, we learned our first kicking move. It was called the **front kick**. To do the front kick, first lift your knee up to your chest. Then straighten the raised leg. You should hit your target with the ball of your foot.

We practiced the front kick as a follow-up move for the basic block-punch combination. First we blocked a punch with the rising block. Then we counterattacked with a right forefist punch. Finally we did the front kick. Mr. Miller reminded me to keep my toes curled back very tightly as I kicked.

We learned another kick as well. It was called the **side kick**. To do the side kick, bend your leg at the knee and bring it up to your chest. Then thrust the leg out to the side of your body. This time, hit your

target with the heel of your foot. Again, it is important to keep your toes curled up. After you have hit your target, return to the bent knee position.

It is important to know a variety of kicks, punches, and blocking moves. That way you can better defend yourself. We learned a new blocking move called the **downward block**. This block is used to defend against punches and kicks to the lower part of the body.

Start the downward block by bringing
your forward arm up across your body. Your
hand is now near your ear. Then swing the
arm down to meet the attacker's punch or
kick. You should hit the attacker with the
soft part of your forearm.

At our next class, we began to learn movements from the first kata. It was fun to practice. I learned new hand and body positions. I really had to concentrate hard to keep all the body positions correct. Practicing the kata helped improve the smoothness of my karate moves.

Mr. Miller said that a kata competition is part of a karate tournament. Contestants are judged on how smoothly, efficiently, and accurately they perform the movements of the kata.

Tournaments also include a **freefighting** competition. In this type of contest, two people throw karate moves at each other as if they were in a real fighting situation. But the contestants must control all punches and kicks. All blows must stop within one inch of the opponent's face and only gently touch the chest or stomach.

The winner of a freefighting match is the person who succeeds in throwing a punch or kick that is not blocked or dodged by the opponent. So you must be alert to defend against the attacker's blows. And you must be able to throw punches and kicks of your own.

As we practiced freefighting for the first time, Mr. Miller told us about a tournament that would be held soon. He said that the best students in our class could compete. I made up my mind to practice hard every day so I would be picked to enter the tournament. Some evenings I practiced with Mom at home.

I worked very hard in my classes, too. I practiced my moves and combinations until they were greatly improved. Each week I learned new moves as well. I felt great when Mr. Miller picked me to be in the tournament.

On the morning of the tournament, I arrived at the gym early. I hurried and put on my gi and began to warm up. Everyone around me was warming up, too. Some students had colored belts on. A few were wearing brown belts. I knew that they must be really good at karate.

The judges called all of the contestants

together to explain the rules of the tournament. The kata competition would be first. Two judges would watch and grade each performance. The freefighting competition would be next. Contestants were divided into weight classes. Then they were paired off for matches. Match winners would compete with other winners until finally there was one winner for each weight class.

I was in the lightweight class. Soon my name was called for the kata competition. I was very nervous. My moves were not as smooth or graceful as they had been in practice. I even forgot to breathe deeply as I had been taught. But I did complete the entire kata without leaving out any of the moves.

The freefighting competition was next. I was squared off against another girl. The referee said, "Ri," which means "bow to one another." We bowed out of mutual respect. Then the referee said, "Begin." We moved in to face one another.

For a moment, I forgot what to do. My opponent flashed a kick at me. I automatically jumped to the side. Then I counter-attacked with a forefist punch. My opponent blocked my punch. She immediately threw a punch right at my stomach. I was not fast enough to block it.

The referee raised his hand and said, "Go to a starting position." He then pointed at the other girl and said, "Winner by one point." We bowed to each other. I was very disappointed. But I walked up to my opponent and congratulated her.

As I walked back to my seat, I felt like a big failure. I hadn't won in either the kata or freefighting competitions. I thought about giving up karate forever.

When the tournament was over, one of the judges came over to me. He was ranked a black belt. He told me that my movements had been very graceful. He said that with practice, I could be a champion one day.

At that moment, I decided I would not give up. After all, this was only my first tournament. Next time I would have a better idea what was expected of me. And I would do better.

I was more enthusiastic than ever. Mom and Dad kept helping me at home. And my teacher helped me in class.

I really improved by the time I entered my next tournament. That day everything went well. I won the beginner's kata competition. And I won two freefighting matches before I lost the third one.

I kept learning new things in class, too. Some of the moves we learned were especially for self-defense outside of class. We learned how to escape from a choke hold. All you have to do is grab the small fingers on each of the attacker's hands. Then pull them away from your neck. This move is more effective if you kick at the same time.

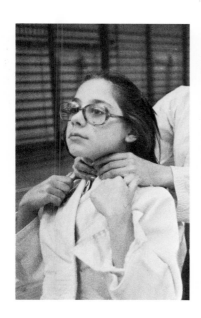

We also learned how to break a hand clasp. If an attacker grabs you by the wrist, just reach across your body and firmly grip your other hand. You can break the attacker's hold by pulling away with both of your hands.

After many weeks of practice, Mr. Miller said that some of us were ready for belt rank promotion. As beginners, we would be eligible for the first colored belt, which is the white belt. All of the belt rank candidates were given a testing sheet. This sheet listed all of the karate techniques we had to perform at the belt rank test.

The test was also to include a kata and a freefighting match. Students would be evaluated on their performances. We would also be required to give a short talk about the history of karate.

I spent a lot of time practicing for the test. I worked extra hard at home until I was sure I could perform all the moves smoothly and gracefully.

The day of the test, I tried to remember the advice my teacher had given me. He said, "Concentrate on your moves, and you won't have time to be nervous."

The candidates for the white belt were tested first. There were twelve of us. When it was my turn to be tested, I assumed a fighting stance.

One of the judges called out some karate techniques. I concentrated on my moves as I performed them. At the end of the techniques test, we were asked to perform the kata. Again we were graded by the judges.

Next we were paired off for our freefighting match. My match was very exciting. I scored on my opponent several times with kicks.

After the freefighting, we were told to sit down. One at a time, the candidates were asked questions about the history and philosophy of karate. When it was my turn, I was able to answer all of the questions. I was happy because I knew I had done well.

At the end of the testing session, the main judge rose to speak. He called out the names of the people in each belt rank group who had passed the test. He called off my name for the white belt rank promotion. The judge handed me a belt, I wrapped it around my waist and tied it. Then the judge and I bowed to each other.

That was a great moment for me. I had worked very hard for my first belt. And I was proud to finally wear it. I began to look forward to my next belt rank promotion. I know I will have to work hard for that one, too. I have so much more to learn about karate. But I am confident because now I know that karate is for me.

Words about KARATE

BELT RANK: A method of classifying self-defense skills according to belt color. The most skilled karate students are awarded black belts. The lowest rank is a white belt.

BLOCK: To use your arms, elbows, or hands to deflect an attacker's punches or kicks

BUSHIDO: The philosophy behind karate, judo, and jujitsu that emphasizes courtesy, self-improvement, and kindness toward others

COMBINATION: Two or more self-defense moves used together in sequence

COUNTERATTACK: To return an attack

DODGE: To move out of the way of an attacker's punch or kick

DOWNWARD BLOCK: A movement to protect against attacks to the stomach and groin

FOREFIST PUNCH: A hand technique using the fist to hit an attacker's body

FREEFIGHTING: A contest between two people who throw moves and defend against attack as if they were in a real fighting situation

FRONT KICK: A powerful foot technique used to hit an attacker

GI: A karate uniform

HOLD: A technique that enables you to contain an attacker and prevent him or her from making any more aggressive moves

JUDO: A sport contest using techniques similar to jujitsu

JUJITSU: A Japanese system of self-defense that is basically defensive rather than aggressive; the gentle art of self-defense

KARATE: An ancient Asian system of self-defense in which the human body is used as a means of defense or as a weapon for attack

KARATE EXERCISES: Conditioning muscles and stretching them to increase strength and flexibility

KARATE TOURNAMENT: A type of competition involving freefighting and kata performance contests

KATA: A prearranged series of karate moves against an imaginary attacker

MODIFIED HORSE STANCE: A stable standing position that is used for self-defense

RISING BLOCK: A type of block that is used to defend against attacks to the upper body

SELF-DEFENSE: The ability to defend against attacks by an aggressor

SIDE KICK: A self-defense kick that is thrown from the side of the body

STRIKE: A quick, snapping attack, usually done with the hand or elbow

ABOUT THE AUTHOR

FRED NEFF has been a student of the Asian fighting arts since the age of eight. He eventually specialized in karate and is also proficient in judo and jujitsu. For many years, Mr. Neff has used his knowledge of the Asian fighting arts to educate others. He has taught karate and self-defense classes in colleges, public and private schools, and city recreation departments. Mr. Neff is now a practicing attorney in Minneapolis, Minnesota.

ABOUT THE PHOTOGRAPHER

JAMES E. REID has been a commercial photographer in Minneapolis and St. Paul since 1969. He is now the director of his own company, Future Vision Corporation, a complete photographic studio and photo processing operation. His favorite assignments are photographing people enjoying the out-of-doors.